Arrivals and Departures

poems by

Stewart Moss

Finishing Line Press
Georgetown, Kentucky

Arrivals and Departures

Copyright © 2024 by Stewart Moss
ISBN 979-8-88838-433-6 First Edition
All rights reserved under International and Pan-American Copyright Conventions. No part of this book may be reproduced in any manner whatsoever without written permission from the publisher, except in the case of brief quotations embodied in critical articles and reviews.

ACKNOWLEDGMENTS

Grateful acknowledgment is made to Plume Poetry, in whose pages "Mid-March" and "The Afterlife of Breath" have appeared.

Special thanks to the following, whose encouragement, support, fellowship and inspiration were of great help to me over the years in bringing this collection of poems to completion: Joseph Bathanti, Grace Cavalieri, Dario DiBattista, David Fountain, the late Rod Jellema, Danny Lawless, V.P. Loggins, the Maryland State Arts Council, Claire McGoff, Leeya Mehta, Nancy Mitchell, Barbara Klein Moss, and Sue Ellen Thompson.

Publisher: Leah Huete de Maines
Editor: Christen Kincaid
Cover Art: *Outpost*, by Jean Halpert-Ryden (1919-2011), from the collection of the author; photo by the author.
Author Photo: John Kaul
Cover Design: Elizabeth Maines McCleavy

Order online: www.finishinglinepress.com
               also available on amazon.com

Author inquiries and mail orders:
Finishing Line Press
PO Box 1626
Georgetown, Kentucky 40324
USA

Contents

Part I

Returned to Carolyn 1
St. Patrick's Cathedral 2
Sunday with Father Flye 3
Watching the Moon Eclipse 5
Parsifal 6
Hearing Glass 8
Cello 9
Entreaty 10

Part II

Written Hopefully 13
For Sophia, for Nathaniel 14
Salad Days 16
Garments 17
Café 19
Meditation on Trouble 21
Words as Freely Falling Objects 22
Responsibility 23
Del Mar 25
Covid Autumn 26
Biography of Wanting 27
Conference Room 28

Part III

Pedestrians on Annapurna 31

Part IV

Beatitude of Oysters Above Tomales Bay 39
Smoked Whitefish 41
Mid-March 42
Castine 43
Ritual Washing 44
Commuting Woes 45

Riding Train No. 6 46
Actually 47
Swinging in Virginia 48

Part V

Sweetness and Mortality 53
Sentry 54
Box of Letters 56
Arrivals and Departures 58
It's Really Truly Trying 59
Motive for Fighting 60
Unpacking 61
There's Always More to Lose 62
The Time of Living 63
Outpost 65
Heroes 67
Weightman 68
Amidah 70
The Afterlife of Breath 71

Notes 72

For Barbara and Sara

Finding myself where I was, I thought—after the journey that had begun so long before—that I was blessed.
                        V.S. Naipaul, *The Enigma of Arrival*

Part I

Returned to Carolan

Ours is a life of small instruments.
Music blows through the spines of books,
strings stretch along the walls in smoke
and in the placement of things
are songs of stillness.

A ladder back chair faces a white window
and attends to the light,
a ram's horn is coiled to bleat alarms
and in a photograph an old priest
who is almost deaf
stands at his door of memories,
his hands clenched
to shake a voice from air.

Carolan, your harp is true,
your blindness reaches me
through your fingertips.
Just enough sound to make
the silence settle deeper,
and I hear the smoothed objects
waiting to be used.

St. Patrick's Cathedral

A sculpted pore that dilates
on warm days,
admitting walkers, the makers of prayers

and the curious, who wish to gaze
at earnestness. I enter dazed,
thinking I am shoeless in Florence

and want only to glide on marble
and breathe in shadow.
Candles stand vigilant by collection boxes

and flash on coins that slide
from white fingers.
In a corner confessionally dark

a passion is enacted—
one figure leans toward another,
lips burst red at their touching.

Incense rises to eyelids
along rows polished by waiting.
Supplicants do as they're told—

press back their spines
and behold. Light flies
through glass gratings,

I want to kneel and ask questions.
Others are randomly pausing, pausing.
In shadow comes suggestion.

Sunday with Father Flye

In his photograph, the clerical cloth
and wooden door behind merge
in one dark hue. Hair and face are white,
the thin line of collar is poised
on its rounded edge as if to dip forward

and cuffs hold hands that are large, bare,
lightly tensed, offered out.
His eyes seem startled by some brightness
beyond the frame, though it hangs
on a quiet wall pale from a drawn window shade.

Seated in his room behind the door,
we talk long into the looping day,
each second revolving, drifting off,
stirred to its place as seeds are blown
and reappear, reborn and multiplied,

joined until they drop. I listen mostly
and stroll with him, his eyes turned inward
along intricate tracks etched
by all the stirrings in the world
that came his way and come again.

It is not forgetfulness that makes him pause
but what is as close a breathing.
His ear is pressed to what beats inside the head
and grows sharper further back,
like the Latin texts he read at school,

loud and clear in the historic present.
He is not lost, this teacher, but always led back
to the giving, to the voices still beating
urging him to speak for them.
So Agee speaks, line by breathing line,

set free by Father's lips and tongue,
precise as chisels then silent as a finished stone.
He pats the books once, twice

as he lays them on his desk,
as if rousing Rufus' head dozing on his shoulder

on the train to Paris in the '20s.
Postcards sealed in cracker tins stacked
against the closet's rear wall
were fresh then from kiosks and hotel stands,
were scored on the backs

from the rush of first seeing:
Gothic slabs massive in dreams,
Mont St. Michel hovering at high tide,
washing over Tennessee trees.
He still feels the weight upon his shoulder,

the apprehension of intensity
brilliant but unbearable,
a smoldering brilliance, and here as he traces
and retraces, his splayed fingers flying
in restless urging again

as they clap together and slap
the dark crippled knee.
Well, well, well, he cries, his eyes lit
by small fires, *my soul and body!*
now mingling in mystery,

the second bending into the first,
reaching out in strong hands hooked
to the spine.
And I am pulled beyond myself
into that same startling light

outside all frames,
where elusive tracks of memory
gather, blaze up, disappear
and drift as haze
down the long, inward, peopled gaze.

Watching the Moon Eclipse

Standing in damp grass beneath the star-spotted sky,
alive with the blinking of satellites and planes
and the rich dramas of our dreaming,
we watch the moon as the sky swallows it slowly,
and while the moon slides into the sky's throat and belly,
becomes the dulled vermillion of a frost-blighted orange,
and the sharp August wind scrapes down from Monadnock
riffling the grass, our hair and the thin tent behind us,
our daughter presses more closely to me and trembles,
begins in her chest a deep sobbing of terror
as the moon throbs in grimey neon,
contracts within its own penumbra,
and absconds into the black alchemy of its beginning,
making us small ones know that only change
is fixed in the stars.

It is all too much for her.
She turns and crawls into the tent,
snuggles inside the billowing softness of feathers,
clutches the kindred carcass of her bear and sleeps—
a chick under a hen's wing,
lost in the down of forgetfulness,
lost in the blackness beyond dreaming.

And it comes to me as I stand beneath the moon's closed lid
that ontogeny may very well recapitulate philogeny
and the sobbing child is a shaman of our almost lost past
who dances and chants by starflight to placate the darkness
and make the moon reappear as a bubble floating
amidst its shimmering borrowed light.

As my wife and I curl close to our daughter's sleeping
and shiver in the tent flapping its hollow music
blown loose by the mountain's breath,
I wave my hand across the moon—
the moon that shows us all we have to lose
when it disappears—
in benediction of the light that calls us together
and of the darkness that draws us apart.

Parsifal

In memory of Charlie Stone

Whenever I hear Wagner on the radio,
some of the worst music ever written—
monotony of percussive violence,

strings swelling with self-pity,
trumpets flaring with scorn—
and reach to turn it off,

I pause and think
of Charlie's love of opera, even Wagner,
his allegros of librettos over coffee at work,

his sotto voces of pleasure and arias of delight.
His tongue stained raspberry from the jujubes
he popped all day to fuel his frenetic joy,

he soloed into me an expectation, brief, of grace.
As on the Good Friday we saw *Parsifal* at the Met,
a damp wind hurtling us down Broadway

as we dashed to make the final call.
I dozed high above the fray,
my forehead pressed against the cool brass rail,

and missed the Grail, almost missed Klingsor hurling
the glowing spear, when Charlie jabbed my ribs
just as the spear took flight—

O suspended shaft of light—
and the bright gasp in Charlie's eyes
when Parsifal stretched up to snag it.

To hold the light in one's hand or in one's eyes
as it flashes out through the darkness of memory
is to want what is, then is not, then becomes something other,

a raspberry liquor that rains on the souring earth
and on the dead no sacred spear can heal.
Rains even on the bones of Richard Wagner,

who gazes sightless at the silent stars
and opens his clenched, chalky jaws
to taste.

Hearing Glass

I am listening to Phillip Glass,
        the music of *Koyaanisqatsi* a long tunnel
where sounds are birthed, a moaning
        of wind, or a kind of muted singing
that announces the entry of notes,
        each of them adorned with feathers and beads
and balancing on their heads
        woven baskets overflowing with ripening fruits.
Monuments of stone shout their stillness
        in stolid resistance to thunder
and all that rushes forward
        to mark the torrent of time.
In a church once, where wooden beams
        above our heads formed the "A" of "And …."
I heard a young man play the *Etudes,*
        as if teaching himself
and all of us in the audience
        the lessons of sound,
the guts of the piano surging
        with his fingers, like the ebb and flow
of the ocean in a race to dissolve the distance
        between our heartbeats.
Hearing Glass that way was like looking
        through a windowpane
after the rain, as the dripping stopped
        and a clay bowl of silence waited
to be filled.

Cello

As if the trees have conspired
to shape a body that sings

the way they dreamed the wind
would someday make them sing

when they were there
at their own birth

and the first roots murmured downward
through the loamy dark

searching for a voice—
worm mutterings, guttural groans of moles,

bones caked with the memory
of their mortal music,

their instruments crushed and un-played,
then bass layers of iron

heavy with gravitas and grief,
rivulets oozing black octaves

and molten pools wailing to escape.
So when the cellist sets her fingers to the strings

like high-wire dancers that prod the air
and strikes with the swift Aeolus of her bow,

the earth recalls the secret music
written on the staff lines of its buried strata,

the grateful trees quiver their choruses,
veins and limbs swollen with sound,

and birds cling, wavering,
then scatter in applause.

Entreaty

When Egyptians believed the tongue to be the rudder
that steers the soul into the next world,
where tellers of pious tales emerge from their wrappings
to an applauding sun and liars are ravaged
by three-headed beasts,
I hope they were including my cat Hamish,
whose chirrups of joy at the utterance of his name
and weeping threnodies for a closed bedroom door, an empty bowl
bespeak goodness and righteous indignation
and will save him, surely, if only the gods allow.

Sentinel over silence, he roams the empty hallways
sending forth a shrill alarum at the faintest rumble
only he can hear. Serenader of lovers, he countertenors
our deepest moans with his querulous wailings,
recalling fecund nights that beckon him no more,
or his years on the prowl when a fat cardinal perched
on a low branch was flesh for hunting,
not an idea for pondering from the soft grass
beneath the flowering dogwood tree.

Prophet of equilibrium, he purrs when light comes
and when light passes, purrs
to Mozart and to Muddy Waters, purrs
on my lap as I write these verses
the middle C hum the earth may make
as it wobbles blindly along its course, rudderless
except for a whirring, a thrumming in the mute darkness,
a rubbing against air, a throbbing, a purring.

Part II

Written Hopefully

If there is hope it is more
        than we have yet understood,
more than any longing noble or not,
        that what is wanted to happen will happen,
and the light that flickers at the edge of breath
        will not be consumed.
Try to draw close to me, my love,
        though I know you strain ahead
away and away, come back
        and press your shoulder to mine
to my powdery moth wing,
        we flutter slowly
poised to fly, blind
        into the blankness of the air.

For Sophia, for Nathaniel

> *All I had to show, as a man of letters, were these few*
> *tales and essays, which had blossomed out like flowers*
> *in the calm summer of my heart and mind.*
> —Nathaniel Hawthorne, "The Old Manse"

1

Her pregnancy, she says, is the poetry of discomfort,
her belly filled with words unspoken
but humming in the darkness a tune
of water thickening, the surface tense
just before the first mouth breaks through
and gasps the sweet hot air.

2

Squash blossoms burst from thin green tubes
down the slope, among the reeds
and lapis spires of pickerel weed,
her husband rises from the river
to the thudding sun,
his body a white form,
his back hair in flourishes.

There is something more awful
in happiness than in sorrow,
for those who rise must vanish
and all must vanish,
leaving only their outlines
sketched on the air.

3

In the shallow river, Nathaniel strains
a bath from the mud.
He imagines these hot days
as a throat scratched
by stories struggling together
in a dry passage of escape.

He dresses and sees the peach tree
and knows he cannot write.
The slender branches bent so heavy
with their fruit are arches
of ripe light supporting the air,
and the bulging peaches cannot hold
all that is given them, and depart.

4

The window can barely hold the words
he carved with her diamond
in the gold light—*the smallest twig leans clear
against the sky*—the double lines blurring in a streak of sun
and pale against the black ash and willow
and the clapboards smudged with moss.

Nathaniel swallows the dust the day offers,
climbs to the house and takes back
his wife's hand.

5

That night is water. He takes her hand
and writes with it in the air
the word spoken by all hands
when they reach out for another's,
and returns with it through the glassy shadows
with the boney weight crouching cool
in his writer's hand,
the weight of peaches falling,
the weight of words bumping moth-like
against the old, dazed windowpane.

Salad Days

Don't move, don't move,
        just the way you are—
                your neck exposed,
your thin shoulder bones
        winging out
                and pressing the air
beneath your gauze shirt.
        How could I ever think you other
                than what you are?
This night, by this candle flame,
        the angle of your body
                intersecting the light just so,
below the falling leaves
        as I wait
                beneath your wings.
Come from the tree
        with its branches
                that have multiplied for years
against the darkening sky,
        where each muffled star
                calls you away,
far from this table of corn,
        and lettuce thickening
                in oil pressed from the fruit
of other trees.
        If you would come
                I would catch you,
gazing inward though I am,
        my delicate shouldered one.
                Come, fall, be with me,
let me unfold you.
        Hold me close
                this cold night.

Felchville, VT, 1982

Garments

Just beyond the inner sanctum of the dressing rooms,
I sit quietly in a wicker chair, caught
between boredom and the edge of meditation

and gaze at skirts and trousers,
camisoles and other bright apparel displayed
like the banners of some lost Gnostic order

that worshipped nakedness with such fervor
its devotees could only bear to know it by the garments
the dazzling flesh shed before becoming pure light.

Within their booths, my wife and others
button and unbutton, bend and wriggle,
step into and out of

in a choreography of confession
before mirrors that are patient, mute, but not unjudging—
cool plates of coated glass reflecting

palimpsests of youth with its remnant taut lines,
while the body becomes dust
or merely becomes itself.

As sales staff smile at me solicitously,
portering their loads lithely back and forth,
their arms dripping with colored cloth,

I, too, want to strip the clothes from my body,
hurl my belly to the ground like King Saul
and wail and prophesy against my foes.

Or whirl with poet doctor Williams
in a private *danse russe,*
my blanched flanks singing in the north room's glare.

The genius of nakedness is its rebuke of the enemy,
like bare stars in darkness
that only blindness can conceal.

Outside, plackets of grey cloud peel and drift away
as the sky slowly, slowly
unbuttons its blouse to us.

Café

When she asked me
what my poems are about,
I answered words, music

and the complexities of desire.
My coffee was suddenly bitter,
as if my tongue were in stocks

exposed to stoning
and the pecking of birds.
The room hushed

but spoons clinked and scraped.
Desire? she asked and tossed her head
like ravens taking flight.

What kind of desire?
Restraint and longing, I said,
linen and nakedness,

duty and the flesh.
The table between us narrowed
then widened,

years diminished then gathered
in heavy folds.
She glanced at my hair—

a gray rumpled cap—
and then at her watch.
I'm late, she said, and stood to leave.

Outside the lettered window
the day darkened.
Inside, footsteps struck

in hollow syllables.
A door opened then closed,
and a sharp draft entered like a breath

that is exhaled
and freezes in air.
A caesura.

Meditation on Trouble

A candle flickers in a hut,
        and a young man scratches out
                the first dim words of a poem
on a piece of slate,
        the fire fading and smoking.
                His thoughts reach out to branches,
which stretch into the invisible air.
        How could this elixir of words fail to intoxicate
                like the dampness he discovers
in the freshly mown grass?
        His poem is the artful imposition of happiness
                that sees also the ripples
                        of its own vanishing.
I remember the naked fingers
        of a woman I once loved,
                the feathery hairs delicate shafts
of pure light,
        when she turned to me and said,
                I have a grievance against you
that will never be forgiven.
        In the ripeness of years
                is it crazy to write
like there's no tomorrow,
        to forbear all darkness
                in these times of trouble?

Words as Freely Falling Objects

The gravitas of words is negated
in their free fall through space.
Feathery nouns riffled by desire
like *nape,* blue *pulse, down* of thigh,
and the heavier ones we empty from our pockets like stones—
loss, failure, pain, oblivion—
plus words from instruction manuals, cereal boxes, annual reports,
words that newspapers never print,
all fall together as their castaway selves.

Falling words have no priority list,
no proclamation of most favored,
no winners of awards or gulags for the damned,
no beautiful ones basking on sunny isles
sipping drinks by dazzling pillars,
no expletives sprayed on brick
then expunged with public money.
No rhetoric to bind them in elegant logic
that expects a vast applause.

Certain gestures do linger on the skin.
Actual touches and caresses rub
with the whorled ridges of their unique imprinting
and leave an aroma delicate as evaporating mists
that rise in recognition when the beloved passes nearby.
But words plummet in flights of dispossession,
far removed from larynx and tongue, from ink,
from electronic throbbings that click and click with fervor
when cease when the hands withdraw.

Even when you say someone's name,
as I said her name long ago by the river
to heal her of a mute sadness I never understood
and kissed her fingers stained red from pistachio dye,
stigmata of her solitude,
salty and raw in the early spring wind,
even then you know that eyes cannot hold a word long,
will only sparkle, briefly, before darkening
and are holes through which words flee
in their free fall away.

Responsibility

for Bruce Katz

Surrounded by books about mountains,
I sip mint tea in a bookstore
and look out at a mountain,
the pines precarious along the ridge,

skiers hurtling like grains of sand
tumbling down a dune,
and remember the talks we had
in the mountains.

How assumptions must be stripped
from how we speak
and preconceptions raised like shrouds
from some pure body of thought

that yearns to arise in ecstasy
and lead us back beyond the darkness
of our words.
Responsibility, you said, means only

being able to respond,
as if it carried no moral weight
and conscience were a crystal
melting into air.

But where to begin,
what meanings abandon first?
Which ones exiled to the void
of some pure imagined past?

They cluster in waiting rooms,
where piles of magazines are dog-eared
from the dead century,
and listen for the song that summons them back—

a note sounding like desire,
when the body plunges forward

to grasp the life it can never have,
even as words fail

and exhaust themselves, emptied and dry,
and wants only the flush of arrival,
a spraying burst of snow
and the heart responding and, yes, wanting more.

Del Mar

On the deck at *Kirby's*, waffles bulge
on white plates, drip boysenberry syrup
and chunks of fruit plucked when heavy
from dense rows of local shrubs.

Hibiscus has never blossomed redder,
nor the Pacific swelled with such bosomy sighing,
yet we know we can never possess it
in this land where possessions reign.

So we blame the lithe blonde waitress
for this ungraspable abundance,
blame the blue sky, the blue water for their blueness
and the pelican for its bulge-billed gliding,

blame the graceful bathers for their beauty,
and the ungainly for the specks
their steps deposit in our eyes.
Our coffee could be stronger and we blame

our tongues for their jaded coating,
blame the past for its withered ripeness
and the future for its bobbing
just beyond the horizon's rim.

We see that our plates are empty
except for stains of sunlight
and the sticky, gritty leavings
of our chewed and swallowed blame.

Covid Autumn

Even mixing green beans
        with a mustard vinaigrette
                for Shabbath dinner,
I still recall just days ago
        how the gulls glided weightless
                over the creek,
and the muted colors of late autumn
        called attention to everything
                but themselves,
yet how the joy I felt was subdued
        by my intellectual gaze,
                and I questioned
how such beauty could exist.
        But then it came to me,
                as swift as wings and the breeze,
never to interrogate joy,
        or begrudge anything so free
                that it carves its life
out of the sky
        even as the winter chill and heavy shadows
                intrude.

Biography of Wanting

It was winter, late afternoon. Snow
coated the holly leaves outside,
the berries glinted. He sat
in an empty room and wanted nothing,
as if each breath were exhalation only
blown into a gathering beyond him
of aspirates becoming song.

He wanted neither the cities he had loved,
their streets filled with clamorous passion,
their rivers silver and gull-pecked,
their towers and minarets pressing hard
against a membrane of sky, nor the shared crust
of yellow bread on Friday, nor the salt
from his daughter's fingers.

He saw that it was night and did not know,
or want to know, if the snow
had melted or was invisible in darkness.
He stood up and climbed the stairs to the woman
whose silent wanting called him to bed,
as if arms could call to him they wanted,
but her arms he did not need.

He undressed and crawled inside the billowing folds
where she reached to hold him,
lest he drift up into the thick clouds
that would welcome him as a fugitive brother,
teach him the cold alchemy of un-wanting
then release him to fall crystalline, silent and unseeing
back into the wanting world.

Conference Room

After we check our rancor at the door,
garrison our egos
but keep them on alert,

we drag our chairs to the table
and conjure a rapt earnestness
from the pallid window-light

that haloes our heads,
mutter, *Yes, I agree*, or *Let's consider that later*,
but then for a moment,

perhaps from dim memories
of childhood circle games—
spin-the-bottle, duck-duck-goose—

our faces forget themselves,
settle more deeply
into who we were,

the tissue radiant with recognition
of our oldest, closest friends,
who cavort, steal a kiss,

understand that now
is all we have.
When embarrassed by this nakedness

that catches us off guard,
we resume our sober masks,
glance, slanted, at the clock,

set our pens to yellow pads
and turn once more
to the business at hand.

Part III

Pedestrians on Annapurna

> *In October 1978, a team of nine women climbed Annapurna in the Himalaya of Nepal. Two died.*

1. Arlene speaks

How can I separate the mountain
from the one who gave me my first climb?
Sometimes his eyes were the blue firmament
that inhabits thin air
where only the lightest live—
not even clouds but their bones—
luring me with dream of vanishing
spun out forever.

Other times his chest and stomach
were plates of stone,
each seam just wide enough
to wedge a knuckle in
and pull myself up to eye level,
my footholds slipping
in the abandonment of form.

Those days were long and exhausting,
while the peaks whistled quietly and were benign.

But now he is dead,
a victim of himself buried
under tons of ice with two friends
I never met.
You don't conquer a mountain,
you stand at the top quivering
and watch your boot prints vanish in the wind.

So what is it all for
in this world sighing with loss,
its voice the leading edge of silence,
like the geese that honk overhead
in flight south from Tibet and disappear
thirsty for the warm wet land?

I can't say, so I speak with movement,
beginning again like a child
bending into the new world,
each step the first
from deep inside the muscle's throat,
past the fleshy peepal trees
oozing their ripening odor,
past the milky pulses of orchids
dangling like maidens' hands
from the dripping green shrubs.
Past the leeches choked
with our good blood.

I follow the porter's calves,
their blue veins compass needles
slicing brown flesh
that bulges under loads piled high,
baskets strapped to their brows
in medieval toil,
through the villages soaked with tea
and acrid with the butter of yaks,
where children squat in rough cobbled paths
paved by gravity and dogs bark
with the desperation of wolves
fearful of new hunters.

If a face is beautiful
then this land is a face,
though it is creased at thirty-eight
and weighted with goiter
and lives at the feet of this goddess hulk
that shrugs off its stones
with gigantic nonchalance.

Faces smile as we pass,
clustered globes bursting
with their own juice,
amazed at us nine sweating women
without our children and alone, no dowry
hanging golden from our ears,
and we amazed at our own hearts beating,

though we've been this high before
and will climb higher.

We give ourselves to quiet the moaning air,
pitch our tents on a plateau
open to the mountain's shadow,
and take from our many packs and loads
the things of domesticity,
enough for days,
while Sherpa compass us
with sprinklings of herbs and rice,
our walls and our gate,
our meager gleanings from the harvest,
given back in fog and in fire,
in the old stone dreams
that tower in darkness and tremble my legs
in the weariness of sleep.

2. Irene speaks

From Camp V to the summit
there is only breathing and stepping,
six breaths to every step
in a world my goggles filter of sunlight
where every shudder or wind-gust
is cushioned by rubber, by feathers
in which we monsters move,
our brains shrinking
around their polished cores.

It is as if I am dead
and am asked to carry my own body,
as if when the new light comes
I will not rise from darkness.

There is at that moment
on the verge of flight
a final tugging at the body.
The shadow stretches along its full length,
tightens backward like the rope around my waist
and binds me to another.

The weight of her life pulls—
my daughter in her cove of books,
pages exploding in the clarity
of her still new life.

There is hope in images.
The horizon stretches itself
color-less and still,
waiting for the prince, the boys and girls,
the old heroes brilliant on horses
to gallop and prance in a world without mountains,
without the nausea of falling
but rooted to the flat sweet earth.

I know she grows without me,
that should my body fail
she will draw her life
from her own rich bones.

I turn on the summit,
unmask myself and bend
toward the white-capped massifs far below.

This mountain is sustenance.
It is the wild food I feed on
when my life is fenced from me,
absorbed in its own quiet growth.
Full, I begin my descent,
almost too sated to move.

3. Allison speaks

On my thigh there is still a shadow
of some deep fear long ago,
a scar that will not fade.
It grins at me at night
in the roar of falling ice,
in the tent flapping its vacant music.

Today is the last day
this scar will hold me

shaking in the just made light.
It is morning on Annapurna.

Its seamless face turns to me un-furrowed,
dense in crystals,
drawing me out on the steel points
I wear like scalpels
probing the facets' joints.

I am dancing on Annapurna
too fast to make a scratch
until the mountain releases me
and ice closes over me
smooth as flesh.

4. Arlene speaks again

This is a day for bathing,
a day when I undress
and wash myself clean.

The Sherpa look away,
fixed on the flames that burn
our torn tents and other worn gear,
lick high against the mountain's face
and burst the aerosol cans
they throw like bombs
into the fire's round throat.

It is over for all of us. Even now,
I feel my body lose its weight
in this trickle of mountain,
give from itself all the terror
that the mountain gave.

The geese are silent overhead.
Tomorrow they will wade
among the moist reeds
and in the mustard fields waving
their coarse yellow hairs.

The sun delivers its final blow
and it is as if I am fleshless in water,
light as bones.

Part IV

Beatitude of Oysters above Tomales Bay

>*The cure for anything is salt water: sweat, tears or the sea.*
>—Isak Dinesen

Blessed are we who eat oysters slippery with brine
and slide them into our mouths
with greed and gratitude

above the lapis flatness of Tomales Bay.
Blessed is the tongue,
for it seeks out flavor in all things—and not just oysters

but the frothy tang of Lagunitas IPA
and the sweet flesh residing
in the beloved's hidden shallows.

Blessed, too, is Al the shucker,
who pries open each shell with such care
he might be birthing a lamb, or like a potter,

shaping the quivering muscle with his own hands.
Blessed is the white-hulled boat
whose wake bisects the water

and splits in two the heart's grasping, and blessed
is the ocean and the tidal tumult
from which all life springs.

Blessed is the oyster itself,
which, through long forbearance of murk and mud,
pumps them into purity, as if it sees

how much the water means to us
who scud and drift upon it.
For we shall know the sea as a mother

and return to it as if in our own first floating.
The light bulges and blossoms,
galleons of clouds pause in their voyages

and Al raises his knife for a moment,
wipes it on the slickness of his apron
then continues with his delicate laboring.

Smoked Whitefish

> *"If you want to kick sand in the eyes of death, swim the English Channel while holding your breath."*
> —102-year-old gentleman at a deli

In Saul's Deli in Berkeley, California,
pickles and beer jostle for space
with coffee served in heavy mugs.

The waiter's gut seems to swell
with all the dishes the vast menu offers,
while spoons clink and scrape

and jazz bebops through speakers
clinging to walls papered with old photos.
The wizened old guy teeters above me

gripping his cane, his knuckles
white on the table for balance,
his face fiercely red

and his plaid shirt billowing like the robe
of a prophet descending a mountain.
I chew my smoked whitefish and wonder

how it, too, had eluded death
until its life was ended
by a hook or net.

It glistens on my plate,
half-eaten and long gone,
salty testimony to the pointlessness

of holding your breath too long,
or having gills, supple fins
and a strong, muscled, glittering tail.

Mid-March

after W.C. Williams

If, when I sit here in my study
        on a March afternoon,
the pink cherry tree out the window
        rapturous in the late day sun,
my feet resting on a kilim cushion perched
        on a pulled-out desk drawer,
a modest glass of spirits by my elbow
        the closest I can come now
to the schnapps my bubbeh failed
        to carry back to the shtetl
when the distiller saw she had bare feet
        and sent her to the cobbler instead
to buy herself some shoes,
        and my mouth watering at
the pickled herring I'll serve later
        to my wife and myself,
and maybe build a small flame
        in the fireplace crusted
with the charred soot
        of our laughter and our longings,
who shall say
        I am not the happy genius
of my household,
        though I do not dance to admire
my bare flanks, face, arms and buttocks
        in the cloudy bedroom mirror,
but whirl instead to upset
        darkness and celebrate
the swelling bosom
        of the rising gibbous moon,
what the shamans have told us since long ago
        is the sign for gratitude.

Castine

Narrative lies at the heart of poetry
        until it's overwhelmed by language
                and the glitter some words shed.

Yet I give them to you knowing
        that inside is a story, a consciousness
                moving forward with the wind.

Don't be distracted by the faint voices wafting
        through the open window,
               for they unravel the silence and make images clear,

like the gull perched on a solitary rock
        at the edge of the rising tide.
                Then the undulating fields and summer pines,

white clapboard houses with their brave little gardens
        growing zucchini and spangled ears of corn.
                Always the boats and glimpses of the bay,

sometimes a heron lifting skyward
        dragging its skinny hinged legs.
                Don't you realize the sea has a voice

that can't be quelled—
        not by the setting moon, the ebb and flow of darkness
                or the flotillas of stars casting nets

for lost worlds? Another truck rumbles by,
        gears grinding up the hill. Nothing satisfies
                like stillness—it redeems a wasted morning,

offers a blue canvas for swift contrails of thought,
        where the story begins in one unpainted corner,
                flashes across the sky like lightening,

or the first flickers of fire your tongue ignites.

Ritual Washing

A mother walks with her daughter
        on the beach. Their hands swinging
                into air and casting off the day,

and their feet stepping in easy unison,
        they arch their necks against the sky
                in a kind of ritual washing

that birds do late in cities,
        diving low over parks
                and skimming standing pools.

They go in cleanness,
        thinning blood with movement
                as painters make colors pale with white.

And mother in her grey cardigan,
        worn raspberry skirt, and t-shirt
                of north sea green eddying and foaming

over her breasts, her knitted socks
        and her sneakers the ones used
                by sea people here,

and her faded hair held tight
        in coiled lines, sees me as a spot
                upon the eye, breaks stride

and then walks on to her daughter,
        who walks ahead.
                Boats are at rest, boats are under sail,

Long Island disappears in smoldering haze
        and the day enfolds itself, scrubbed and cool
                in the smudging night.

Commuting Woes

It is the same morning labor of footsteps,
        barefoot to shower, rubber-soled to car,
                kicking with reluctance at gas pedal and clutch

past the marsh, the stucco church deserted
        before the early mass. Then scraping to the platform
                and taking my place in the usual huddle

rumpled as I am, among the sleek tycoons and execs,
        the smooth operators with leather satchels
                recalling the pony express and our nation's best

in whooshing speed and grace. I stare blandly
        at the tracks, waiting for the ruby sun to rise
                behind the local bank. It is too early

for battle, not early enough to run away,
        a thought I wonder if I share with Ed
                (Mobil Oil, silver hair)

who often greets me genially, tells me
        of his weekend cruise in the most laconic way—
                What a wind to Port Jeff, had to beat like hell

the whole way back, got drenched! his eyes
        becoming sails the closer the train gets.
                The lights bear down. I step uncertainly on deck.

Riding Train No. 6

Through a window a brown hedge
beneath a bituminous sky,
the moon sallow

and pocked, the birds silent
and concealed,
the coach careering onward

as smoke gathers,
wolves bay
and darkness hulks

on the horizon.
This is where you go
when there's no place left

to leave, all the tickets
have been sold
and the rails set adrift,

and rust beckons
with the enveloping arms
of your long-lost red-haired lover,

who always knew you'd wander back
to where you started
in the end.

Actually

Two young boys on the town green discuss how they'll spend their day. The one who sits against the trunk of a maple, poking for treasure amid the thick grass, says, *Actually,* and then something I can't quite hear. Is he mimicking what his parents say when they sort through the vagaries of their lives, searching for what they can touch and hold? As opposed to, say, the virtual world in which so much of their lives is spent?

Did I ever use that word when I was eight, and did anything virtual exist back then? Yes, there were the stories caught within the paper pages of books, and the dreams of running free across an endless meadow, then leaping off a bluff to glide to a beach below, where driftwood is clumped like ancient bones and the sea roars its singular song. Time held its breath then—it didn't rest but explored its own capaciousness.

The concrete soldier with his musket ready stands as a memorial to the town's Civil War dead. His is a silent and hollow call that bores its way back to the irretrievable, a bugle blast that no one hears. The boy rises and turns away from the clapboard schoolhouse behind him, looks down at the harbor below and steps forward into the glittering, actual world.

Swinging in Virginia

The aromas of closeness gather
in the morning heat,
earth sweats upon itself
and mingles its fragrance

with all who live here.
The earless dog dozes
by the bed, its jowls
hung with drool

the color of old ice melting,
it sprawls among
the scattered toys and clothes,
a randomness I want to order

but, as a guest, cannot.
Outside, I hear the creaking
of sticks tolling
a child's swinging tugs.

Back and up
toward the sucking sun,
he rides hooked to a wooden bridge
bleached as an old rib

heaved out by the slow shudder
of the earth as it lumbers
along its own blind course.
Through the screen flecked

with the bodies of lunging moths,
I see the swing, trapeze, wooden horse
and the almost horizontal boy
caught with hair whipped out,

eyes up and wide
against the plunging force,
caught by me over nothing
but caught as possibility

reaching out to the hot nearness
of his spinning world
and the wild swinging
of the clouds.

Part V

Sweetness and Mortality

> *Arise, lift up your hand—*
> *the long night is stifling me.*
> *—Partaw Naderi (translated from the Pushtu)*

The joy of a white bellied hemp flower
that swallows the hot tea of sunlight,
the crooked teeth of the city behind it
gnawing the roasting air

and the crumbling stones bleeding dust.
This was my life in 1972,
zigzagging like patterns in kilim carpets,
dancing one day to the tabla,

the next to the rubab,
footsteps thumping, then a dizzying whirling,
I thought my journey would go on and on.
But when Ahmed plucked his dagger

from where he'd plunged it in the bed post,
pressed its point to the soft flesh
beneath my throat, and said, *You, my friend,*
are a spy sent by Satan,

my mind wouldn't go
where my body was taking it,
and I stepped away from that country
from its sweetness and ruined future,

starlight flickering on the knife blade
the only beacon in the dark.

Sentry

The walls of my body are crumbling
and on the plain barbarians eat their horses
and plot murder for delight.

They see in me an opportunity,
could break through me easily—
but they are in no rush

and are content to laugh
and let the wind blow smoke
against my face.

They have as much right to me
as I do, perhaps even more,
I who believed they would never come

and if they did, would wheel
and spur their horses back
beyond the horizon's edge.

But they are here
and their bellies are strong
with roasted meat.

The nights are long
and filled with their snoring.
They dream of the victory

that is already theirs,
and when they awake roll dice
for the victim's head

and curse the heavens
when they lose.
For me the stars are what they are—

dead light, cold stones, places
that never were.
Dawn drifts back

across my ruins
and the plain clings
to a sheet of mist.

All I have left is the music
in my bones and this grief,
this watchfulness, as I sing.

Box of Letters

The letters whisper in the old shoebox
and the postcards murmur there, too.
They converse in the darkness
of their far-flung lives, what they saw
and the inks and stains they carry—

the cheap Bics from Paris, the cracked Biro
salvaged from the dust in Kathmandu,
the brown splashes of tea
and yellow smudges of curry,
the puckered rings of beer glasses

when I sat amidst gilded buildings
and toasted my life that opened and opened.
I could almost hear the latitudes
and longitudes breathing
and the ancient sighs and moans

upon the breezes. I could smell
the alluring riverbanks,
the mud and fish, the acids of lovemaking,
as I listened to doves cooing in poplars
and pigeons beneath low bridges,

and wrote these letters my father saved.
I read them now and wonder
who held the pen, who licked the stamps,
why I scrawled these messages
from places now in shambles—

Harare, Baghdad, Mazar-I-Sharif—
places the world would just as soon ignore
no matter what witness the letters bear.
Blue and green and faded,
they are a string of bleached prayer flags

that flutter above the crumbling villages,
cast shadows across parched valleys,
and are fastened like ensigns

to the brooding vessels that ply
the deep and turbulent waters.

Arrivals and Departures

Trees bend to what is vacant
and away from their own fullness,
and the grass withers because the sun

has no place else to go.
In this world of arrivals and departures,
does anything remain?

And if the mourning dove
searching for seeds
beneath the purple verbena

finds none, will another bird fold its wings
and coo in consolation?
When Pfc. Dixon was shot

from the ragged Helmand hilltop,
the clouds had fled and the flowering tamarix
shimmered in the absence of wind.

The grass still burned because the sun
had nothing to hide it,
and the dove pecking for seeds

struck a stone and flew up
in a burst of feathers.
Yes, Dixon thinks, there goes my heart,

and, no, oh no,
I am not going with it.

It's Really Truly Trying

It's really truly trying
  dealing with my brain.
It follows paths I never knew I had—
  the flashes that can't be flushed from memory,
the harsh ripening of the moon
  over a dusty plain,
the aftertaste of darkness
  on the tongue.

It's truly hard
  dealing with my brain
when it spins on its own axis
  or explodes like a celestial event
so that stars are blurred, feet
  feel like stones, and the yelling and smells
bring me to my knees.

My brain skitters and shudders
  along its own blind course,
like a crazy dog chasing its tail
  in a cyclone of sand,
or a wounded deer lurching
  across an empty road.
Or a bird flailing in a fierce wind,
  as it holds fast to the one life
it can't escape.

Motive for Fighting

The reason I went over there
was to keep it all

from the people back home.
The chaos and fire

and indifferent darkness
that shrugs dumbly

at your prayers.
The days that claw at you

with bullets and exploding dirt,
as if the ground were revolting

against a violation it couldn't name.
I wanted to engulf all this

within myself, like a canister welded
to carry toxic wastes,

or a volunteer paid to test a lethal drug,
or a goat whose flesh is pierced

with tiny flags bearing sins
we don't even understand

and is cast out into the wild,
where wolves wait for it to stumble

and hawks tear at what is left,
then, gorged and content, fly back

to the rough-hewn nests
that are their homes.

Unpacking

The best part, I thought, would be the vacancy
I returned to, how I could fill it
with whatever heavy burdens I carried
and walk away lighter, more erect.

I remember those first hours—
the sky neutral, blank with clouds
and unencumbered by the blue
so often pasted to its gut.

The way the stairs mimicked
the steps I took on patrol,
then ended at a door that opened
to a barren darkness.

The chore of unpacking lasts forever.
The clothes with their stories
of sweat and escape. The thick extra sweater
the Afghan cold abused.

Then the emptiness that can't be lifted out
and tossed on a bed. If joy or hope
or even a fragment of clarity are hiding
in the creases of that bag,

I haven't found them yet.
So what was vacant remains
and finds its resting place
inside my own heart.

There's Always More to Lose

There's more to lose than yourself—
the sun a yellow flower bursting
in an overheated room,

clouds unspooling along flyways
against a seamless swatch of blue,
a door opening to a candle flickering

on a table and a bottle of wine
drunk on its own redness,
and the flesh of her leg

that asserts itself from the table's shadows.
There's more than yourself to lose,
you, who are a climber high into the air

beyond any cooling mist
and the soothing whoosh of feathers,
or the warmth of flesh

that proclaims itself
from beneath the table and stretches out
like a cat, saying pet me, make me purr,

before you lose yourself,
before the full mass of your body
drags down only part

of what you have to lose
and, too late, you know
that you are lost.

The Time of Living

When the soldier's young wife was asked
what has been lost, she answered only
with fluent silence. Then, *I want to go back
to the time of living,* she said,
and looked away from all our faces.

I wondered what that time of living was—
a place where streams were silver
with their own arriving?
Where hawks floated above the pines
and smooth stones paved a path to clarity?

Where waiting was a kind of blessing
as pickerel shimmered among the undulating weeds,
and his body endured like the pebbles
she still carries in her pocket
and quickened with the wind

that raced down the hillside and riffled his hair?
This was before his skull was encased in a helmet
and expanded into a fragile roundness,
his eyes flashing with the bursts of shells
and exploding with the sunlight.

On night patrol, sharp stars
etched trenches in the darkness and constellations
sang the ancient stories that sprayed like fire
from a dragon's mouth.
Back in the time of living, the solid earth

held them both, then their son
and their daughter. They could hear
one another's hearts twang in cadence
to the night's pulsing.
His hands were soft but strong,

open and never clenched in fists.
When he took her in his arms
and kissed her, his tongue searched hers

for its pliant wetness
and the sweet mists of her breathing.

He has kissed her only once
these past six months,
a dead, cold kiss like a snake lying coiled
inside a dark hole, afraid of the light
that seeps in from long ago

when all their time was for living.
If she goes back now, she steps quickly
and leaves no footprints
so no one knows
she was ever there.

Outpost

In memory of Jean Halpert-Ryden

In your picture of a village
that might be in Galilea,
the green and brown hills

reach down in sloping layers
to the olive grove
behind the clustered white houses.

Two boys perch on a bicycle
as if gravity were no object,
and a child takes shelter

against her mother's broad hip.
Three slouching youths stare
in three directions,

lost in resignation
while a small car points its exit
down a ridged dirt road.

From where you sit now, Jean,
inside your barren outpost
of plaque and tangled fibers,

the road runs through a world
that could, for all you know,
be a painting, or through a painting

that is the world.
Have you forgotten
what the brush is for,

and do you remember
when the strokes came like speech
as you explored

the mystic realm of color?
The clouds you fixed
like knotted muscles

in the sky, or the whites of eyes
that will not close,
wait for you to answer.

Heroes

> *All the proud fathers are ashamed to go home.*
> *Their women cluck like starved pullets*
> *Dying for love.*
>   —James Wright

How good to be a young football player
after a hard practice
whose girl leads him by the arm
to her shiny red car,

and drives him past the big stone houses
with their many windows and iron gates
and the maples flushed and full
before their long nakedness.

He admires her tanned legs and the strong hands
that have gathered him to her,
and the way she turns to him and smiles, calmly,
in the rumbling silence

as if she knows his bruises will be healed,
all his failures forgiven.
Or say the road runs past
the crumbling factories and peeling mills

of a small town in southeastern Ohio
that sheds its rust and sorrows
into the brackish river.
The stadium above the river is quiet

for all the young men have gone
and only the battered ghosts of their bodies
gallop against each other in the wind,
which sounds from time to time

like a girl's laughter
that is easy, without fear,
and then like a distant sighing
when her laughter ends.

Weightman

for my father

The first one was a lump of stone
we found half-buried in Slotnick's field.
Scraped of mud and dried
in the April sun, it weighed in my hand more
than I'd hefted before,
made my body lurch to the right,
nearly threw me to the ground
as I pushed it out,
watched it wobble feebly and bounce
at your feet.
You hopped away, like someone on his day off,
fatigue still clinging to your shoes,
glad to be surprised by anything voiceless
as a stone.

Later you regaled me with old clippings,
held each one by its browned edge,
your old long name the winner
again and again. Your look glazed
around a fragment of memory
caught between thumb and finger:
it was that fragile,
the way a man tells you how close
he almost came
to shouldering a burden for good
and straightening it up.

On Nazing Street in Dorchester, 1926,
a boy thick through the chest
heaves his mother's iron
at the backyard fence. The neighbors
wonder at the crashes,
mutter over copper basins
foaming with broth,
glad he isn't theirs.

An iron ball I pushed for years,
hurled it ritually every spring in fresh mud,
splattered your old pants,
watched you hop away.
The day I hit fifty feet
you flicked your cigarette in the air,
marked the pock with a piece of stick, smiled
and looked beyond me
to the hulking edge
of the still heavy world.

Amidah

Whenever my father and I would rise together
      in the old synagogue in Roxbury
            and stand in silence for the meditation

muttered by the men who encompassed us
      as they bent and rocked within the fringed shawls
           I was still too young to wear,

my father's solid form bundled in one itself
      and smelling of hair oil, cigarettes
           and a peculiar minty sweetness,

I would press the heavy prayer book against my chest
      and feel my heart echo
           among the cryptic, serifed words

that I imagine stood in rapt attention
      to the motes drifting and spinning
           in shafts of light

streaming through the windows'
      star-shaped frames and out
           into the rushing world beyond.

The Afterlife of Breath

My father dead on the gurney
        and yet the nurse urging me to speak to him—
I believe his soul is still here, floating, she said ...
        I wasn't sure about his soul
although I looked for it anyway, a haze
        that had somehow gone from flesh
to mist and dust, but I believed his final breath
        remained. Or maybe it had left him
as he lay on the kitchen floor,
        the bags of groceries he'd carried scattered
as if by a cyclone that had gathered all the breaths
        we mortals have blown out from our own bodies
and may still linger
        in the endless afterlife of breath,
to which every living thing contributes.
        Breath of mind that even in sleep
never stops exhaling its stories,
        and the breaths of clouds declaring their freedom.
The breaths of young voices I heard
        choiring in Soweto, and the Elgonyi elder
who spits on his hands as the sun rises
        and blows out the spray as an offering.
And my own breath as a new father
        when I carried with me
the soft inhalations and exhalations
        of the small being gifted into my arms.
I thought I heard the earth breathe then
        and hear it now, too,
but not without it laboring, not without
        the billions of burdens and arduous gaspings
that cling to its spinning
        in the darkness where we all were conceived
and to which we will return and hum together
        the only song we know of peace.

Notes

page 1

>Turlough O'Carolan (1670-1738) was a blind Celtic harpist who traveled throughout Ireland composing songs. Carolan's "receipts" were often composed and performed in exchange for a dram or two of whiskey and a room for the night. The "old priest" in the photo (taken by David Herwaldt) is Father James Harold Flye, the writer James Agee's teacher, mentor and life-long friend (see p.9).

page 8

>Phillip Glass composed "Koyaanisqatsi" (a Hopi word meaning "life out of balance") to accompany the 1983 documentary that explores how humanity has separated itself from nature.

page 31

>The background for this poem can be found in Arlene Blume's *Annapurna: A Woman's Place* (1980), her account of the first Americans—and first women—to scale Annapurna I, the world's 10th highest peak. Many of the details are from my own time of living and trekking in Nepal.

page 42

>W.C. Williams' "Danse Russe" inspired the structure of this poem.

page 53

>This poem is set on the outskirts of Mazar-I-Sharif, Afghanistan.

pages 58-63

>These poems were inspired by the accounts of active duty members of the military who participated in creative writing workshops, which I attended and in which I took part as a civilian administrator. (The name of the individual in the poem

on p. 56 is fictitious.)

page 65

>This ekphraistic poem was inspired by a painting "Outpost," by
>Jean Halpert-Ryden (1919-2011), which hangs on my
>living room wall, and a photo of which provides
>the cover illustration for this book.

page 67

>The epigraph of this poem is from James Wright's "Autumn
>Begins in Martin's Ferry, Ohio."

page 71

>The Elongyi are a tribe in Kenya.

Stewart Moss has taught literature and creative writing in both the USA and abroad; Scotland, Greece, Zimbabwe, Afghanistan, and Nepal are among the countries in which he has lived and worked. Most recently, he directed a large literary center serving the Washington, DC community and beyond. His poems and essays have been published in journals and books; his chapbook, *For Those Whose Lives Have Seen Themselves* (Finishing Line Press), was published in 2021. He has also been featured in *The Poet and the Poem* podcasts at The Library of Congress and, in 2022, was the recipient of an Independent Artist Award from the Maryland State Arts Council. A native of Boston, MA, he resides in Annapolis, MD.

www.ingramcontent.com/pod-product-compliance
Lightning Source LLC
Chambersburg PA
CBHW020339170426
43200CB00006B/436